SELF CARE
Made Easy

For the Busy Christian Woman:
Make Time for Self-Care and Feel Alive Again

AMA BREW

Cover design by 100Covers

Edited by Nancee-Laetitia Marin, thelanguageagent.com

Formatted by Jodi Salice, highrealmgraphics.com

Paperback ISBN: 978-1-7358224-1-9
eBook ISBN: 978-1-7358224-0-2

DEDICATION

This book is dedicated to all women who are spinning multiple plates, sacrificing daily for their loved ones, and looking for more fulfillment, purpose, and balance in their lives.

You deserve to be well.

TABLE OF CONTENTS

WHO AM I TO WRITE A BOOK ABOUT SELF-CARE?

I know how it feels to be trying so hard to keep up on the outside but struggling with an intense inner turmoil on the inside. It's hard to admit that you don't have it all together when you think that being a superwoman is what makes you worthy and empowered as a woman.

As women, we find ourselves having to wear different hats. We play roles like moms, wives, grandmas, sisters, nieces, aunties, friends, professionals, managers, housekeepers—just to mention a few. We usually find ourselves overstretching and trying to be everything for everybody. In addition, we neglect our emotional, physiological, and mental well-being. This can lead to burnout overtime. As much as we want to do everything and be everything to everybody, we forget that we're just human and can only go so far. Lack of self-care drains us and makes us empty and dry.

After my twin boys were born, my entire life shifted. Even with the birth of my daughter a few years earlier, I'd started to completely lose myself. I was trying to pursue a human resources career, run a home-based business, be the best wife and mom, be a pastor's wife, keep a clean home, and please all other people while neglecting my physical, mental, and emotional wellness. When I realized it was necessary, I eventually left my corporate career and focused on my daycare business so I could care for my kids around the clock.

I stopped doing all the things I loved to do like practicing self-care, writing, motivational speaking, and reading. I'd become so narrowly focused that I couldn't even admit (or see) that I needed help at first.

With time, I felt so tired, exhausted, and unfulfilled. Waking up in the morning was so hard. I was running on fumes. I just hated my existence because I felt I had too many responsibilities than I could handle. I started resenting my life, even though I had almost everything I always wanted. It looked like I couldn't handle my blessing well and the responsibilities that came with it. I kept thinking I should be happy. I have everything I have always wanted—a husband, kids, educational degrees, and a successful business. I looked at myself in a mirror one morning, and I couldn't even recognize myself anymore. That was an eye-opening moment for me.

One day as I sat down, I started reading and researching about my symptoms and feelings. I realized I didn't feel fulfilled because I was so busy trying to look good in people's eyes. I'd neglected very vital areas of my life like self-care, self-development, fun, and recreation. To me these were at the bottom of the list. That's when I realized I needed help. I made the bold step to seek help. This has been one of the best decisions I've ever made for myself.

I'm not writing this book as the woman who has it all together and hasn't faced any challenges. I'm coming to you as a fellow woman who's had struggles with self-care along my journey, yet I succeeded in turning my life around.

HOW TO USE THIS BOOK

This is a journal-style self-help book. Each chapter has an explanation of concepts that will enlighten you about self-care. At the end of each section of this book, there are journal prompt questions that will lead you to do your own introspection and apply the information and knowledge in this book to your own life.

Please don't aim for an overnight transformation. That doesn't exist. There's no magic formula for that. You'll have to apply whatever you learn from this book to your life and decide to do whatever it takes to succeed on this journey.

Don't attempt to do it all at once. Trying to do it all at once will only frustrate you even more. Take it easy on yourself. Read each chapter, work through the journaling activities one day at a time, and allow your mind, body, and soul to be transformed. This is a journey. My journey took me one solid year to reach its peak, and I'm still consciously working on it. Don't expect everything to change in a day, but if you consciously and consistently apply the knowledge in this book to your daily life, you'll reap long-term benefits that will transform your life.

She makes her own bedspreads. She dresses in fine linen and purple gowns.

PROVERBS 31:22

Part One

THE INS AND OUTS OF SELF-CARE

We will delve into self-care, the importance of self-care, and some simple self-care methods you can implement into your already-busy life so you can achieve the wellness you deserve as a woman.

Chapter One

THE WOMAN IN THE INVISIBLE CAPE

I remember how hard life was for me when I thought I needed to be everything for everybody and do everything to perfection to be considered a virtuous woman. I was so busy trying to live up to this picture of the perfect woman that had been set for me as I was growing up.

I'd been told that the best woman was the virtuous woman found in Proverbs 31: a cook, a home manager, a real estate buyer, an investor, a seamstress, the best wife and mom, and a philanthropist. Oh dear, what a perfect woman she was! How I spent years trying to live up to her standards and missing out on one important secret about her! This woman did it all for everyone. She seemed to have been wearing an invisible cape. And so I also wanted to have her cape.

I had the constant need to be busy. I felt guilty when I took time to relax. I had a hard time saying no when others ask for my help, even with my schedule being so full and hard to manage. I strived to be perfect and perform perfectly in all my responsibilities. I had a hard time accepting help. I constantly gave my time and energy to everything else but myself. I exerted energy and effort all the time but made no move to replenish myself. After all, that's what I understood would make me a virtuous woman. As it turned out, I was more of the woman with superwoman syndrome than the virtuous woman.

When a woman feels she needs to do it all to perfection and stretches herself so thin while neglecting her physical, emotional, and psychological health, she may have what is called a superwoman syndrome. The term was first used by Marjorie Hansen Shaevitz, author of the book *The Superwoman Syndrome*.

Women with the superwoman syndrome have the constant need to be busy and feel guilty when they take time to relax. They have a hard time saying no when others ask for their help, even with their schedules being so full and hard to manage.

They don't only take up more responsibilities than they can handle, but they also strive to be perfect and perform perfectly in all these responsibilities, which is impossible. They have a hard time accepting help. They constantly give to others without receiving anything back. They exert energy and effort all the time but make no move to replenish themselves. This was me until I had my aha moment.

Many Christian women today are neglecting themselves and their wellness just because they're trying to live up to the picture created in their minds about who the ideal woman should be. And so they're constantly trying to live up to these unrealistic pictures and willing to neglect their well-being just to attain this level of perfection, which is simply not realistic. This has left many women feeling tired, overwhelmed, stretched, and dead inside.

This is far from what the virtuous woman would do. Inasmuch as she had so many roles, the virtuous woman in Proverbs 31:22 took time off to take care of her needs too: "She makes her own bedspreads. She dresses in fine linen and purple gowns."

I can't believe I've never noticed this about her. Yes, she was busy doing things for everyone, but she still made time for herself and her needs. What a big mistake I'd been making all my adult life! This is why I was struggling with life and not happy. I was overstretching myself in my bid to live up to her standards, but I wasn't doing what she did to care for herself. This is why I'm so eager to share the information in this book with you, my dear reader.

Are you a woman who thinks she has to do it all? Are you trying to raise a family, have a career, serve in your church, keep up your home, attend all of your kids' activities, work out at the gym, and be socially active? Are you constantly on the go? Do you ever give yourself a break?

Do you allow yourself to relax? Do you constantly give, give, give while receiving nothing in return? Do you ever stop attending to the needs of others so you can take time out for you?

If you can identify with any of what I'm describing here, then you made a great choice by picking this book because I want to share with you the strategies and insights I used to get rid of my invisible cape.

Yes, I'm still ambitious and want to achieve many things. Yes, I still strive to be like the virtuous woman, but I have come to realize that her biggest wellness secret was self-care, and so I surrendered my superwoman cape and got on the self-care train to wellness.

You deserve wellness. You deserve a stress-free and burnout-free life. You deserve to be well while you navigate your busy life. The following chapters will guide you to that outcome and transformation.

Journal Activity

Am I exhibiting some characteristics of superwoman syndrome?

_____

_____

_____

_____

_____

Am I neglecting myself?

_____

_____

_____

_____

Do I make time to take care of myself?

_____

_____

_____

_____

_____

Insights

Chapter Two

WHAT IS SELF-CARE?

My daughter was using her iPad one day. After an hour of using it, she ran to me and said, "Mommy, we need to charge the battery. It went off, so I can't use it again." I took the iPad and plugged it in. An hour later, we had a full battery charge. My daughter was happy to be able to use her iPad again.

We need to recharge ourselves as often as we do an iPad. Self-care is making time to take care of your overall well-being. I'm not just talking about getting your nails or your hair done. I'm talking about consistently taking time to refuel yourself.

Many women usually put self-care last on their lists. From experience, I realize we usually have so much to do that we brush aside things that have to do with our well-being.

Many of the women I work with usually use time as an excuse for not being able to take care of themselves. They're either too busy with work, or they're too busy with kids and managing the home. Others also say they can't afford self-care because they're already living on strict budgets.

WHY IS SELF-CARE IMPORTANT?

Self-care is very important because it is the only opportunity we have to reduce stress, which can negatively affect the executive function of the brain.

Stress is how our bodies react to the demands and challenges that we face as people. Stress is defined as "a feeling of emotional or physical tension. It can come from any event or thought that makes you feel frustrated, angry, or nervous."

Research has shown that when we are under stress, our brain stress response takes over, and we go into survival mode or fight-or-flight mode, which makes us act now and think later.

Effects of Chronic Stress

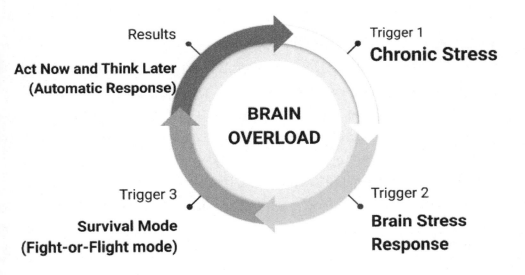

Overload of the brain's capacity for more reflective, intentional responses

When the brain's stress response is triggered, it causes the release of certain stress hormones like adrenaline and glucocorticoids (particularly cortisol). This process leads to certain responses by our bodies such as rapid acceleration of the heart, increased blood flow to the limbs, activation of the immune response, increased blood sugar, and override of the brain's executive function (Babcock 2014).

The executive function of the brain is in charge of our ability to self-regulate, solve problems, set priorities and goals, juggle and multitask, and focus and stick to things.

When the brain stress response is triggered repeatedly by constant stress, it can overload the brain's capacity for more reflective, intentional responses. This is a dangerous place to be because it affects our ability to make clear decisions, set the right goals, set priorities, and make judgments. It also makes us struggle to keep track of problems in our lives, find solutions for dealing with them, and follow a plan for moving ahead.

Overexposure to stress-related hormones and persistently elevated blood sugar also puts us at a higher risk of diseases such as heart disease, hypertension, and diabetes (Babcock 2014)..

The above explanation shows why self-care is important. We need self-care to destress so our brain's executive function can work effectively, resulting in a greater ability to make proper decisions, be able to self-regulate, and handle multiple responsibilities and tasks properly. In addition, as we practice self-care, we reduce our risk for stress related diseases because we decrease the release of stress-related hormones and their effects on the body.

Furthermore, self-care is important because it is biblical:

On the seventh day God had finished his work of creation, so he rested from all his work. And God blessed the seventh day and declared it holy, because it was the day when he rested from all his work of creation (Genesis 2:2–3).

Genesis 2:2–3 makes us understand that God rested on the seventh day after he had created the world. This baffles me when we women, as human as we are, don't see the importance of self-care. God rested and declared the seventh day holy because it was his day of rest. As Christian women, we need to practice self-care so we can rest from all our activities.

Another reason why self-care is important is that it allows us to replenish our lost energy. Lack of self-care drains us and makes us empty and dry. When we keep going and going and going without a break, we get drained emotionally, physically, and psychologically. If we don't spend time refilling and reenergizing ourselves, it results in burnout. This is serious and may take intensive coaching and therapy to recover from.

Burnout is a state of emotional, physical, and mental exhaustion caused by excessive and prolonged stress. Burnout causes people to feel drained, overwhelmed, and exhausted. As much as we want to do everything and be everything to everybody, we forget that we are just human and can only go so far.

After long periods of stretching ourselves too thin, we begin to feel we're running on fumes. We start hating our existence because we feel we have too many responsibilities than we can handle.

We start resenting our lives, forgetting that we brought this upon ourselves. Instead of achieving perfection as we'd like, we'd rather lose ourselves and aren't productive. Remember also that you can't pour out of an empty cup. You can't give out your best if you're empty.

Grab your free Burnout Symptom Check at
http://www.empoweredforbalance.com/burnout

Journal Activity

How important is self-care to my wellness?

_____

_____

_____

_____

_____

_____

_____

_____

Do I make time to replenish myself on a regular basis?

_____

_____

_____

_____

_____

_____

_____

_____

_____

_____

Insights

_____
_____
_____
_____
_____
_____
_____
_____
_____
_____
_____
_____
_____
_____
_____
_____
_____
_____
_____
_____
_____

Chapter Three

BALANCED SELF-CARE METHOD

One of my clients called me one morning, feeling very frazzled. She said she'd made time for herself but still didn't feel refreshed. So I decided to go over her self-care routine with her. After our coaching session, my client realized she'd been caring for only one part of herself—her physical body. She needed more self-care than napping or getting a massage.

She realized she needed to develop a self-care routine covering all self-care areas that every woman must follow. I usually call this the balanced self-care routine. This balanced way of practicing self-care focuses on five very important areas of every woman's life.

You know that self-care is not a one-size-fits-all solution. Therefore, as you start your self-care journey, you need to find how much of each area of self-care you need to incorporate into your self-care routine so you can feel balanced and well cared for.

PHYSICAL SELF-CARE

This area of self-care is important because it affects your health and wellness. It's about taking care of your body. What are you doing to make sure you are healthy? Are you taking time off to allow your body to get the rest it needs to rejuvenate?

Be kind and loving to your body. Understand that you have only one body, and your body is the temple of the Holy Spirit (1 Corinthians 6:19). You need to take care of it just as you take care of the physical building that you worship in. You need to understand that your body is indwelled by the Holy Spirit, so every bad treatment you give to your body grieves the Holy Spirit. God also wants us to present our bodies as living sacrifices (Romans 12:1). So our duty as Christian women is to present a healthy body to God. God wants us to be strong and healthy so we can have the energy to go after our purpose here on earth and live fulfilling lives.

I always say we're like cell phones. When your phone battery drains, you need to plug it into the charger. In the same way, we need to replenish ourselves, or else, we run the risk of burnout and complete shutdown, which comes with other health issues.

You should ask yourself if you have enough sleep or eat healthy, nourishing meals. Do you schedule medical check-ups? Do you groom yourself often?

I know it's hard for us to do any of those things as busy women with many responsibilities and constant struggles, but we must make the effort. Until you change your mindset about self-care and put yourself first, you won't be able to give your best in your work, family life, and relationships.

Journal Activity

Am I taking care of my body?

_____

_____

_____

_____

_____

_____

Overall, how is my health?

_____

_____

_____

_____

_____

What can I improve about my physical health?

_____

_____

_____

_____

_____

_____

Insights

_____

_____

_____

_____

_____

_____

_____

_____

_____

_____

_____

_____

_____

_____

_____

_____

_____

_____

_____

_____

_____

_____

_____

_____

SOCIAL SELF-CARE

Your social life is very important and needs to be nurtured. No one is an island. You need to have a positive support system in place. How often are you interacting with your family and friends? Are you surrounding yourself with toxic people or positive people? Do you have trustworthy people you can call on when times are tough and when you need someone to talk to? Are you spending enough time with people who fill you up and make you feel good?

I'm talking about positive social interaction where you don't have to put on a mask so other people can accept you. You need relationships in which you can just be yourself and express yourself without any fear of ridicule. You must interact with people who see the good in you and are willing to help you become a better person. Don't isolate yourself. Make the effort to connect with people and have meaningful interactions. You must develop a plan to have a positive social life so you can take care of yourself. Positive interactions with people goes a long way to affect your stress levels.

Journal Activity

Who are the three people I can
depend on in times of trouble?

_____
_____
_____
_____
_____
_____

Are the people in my inner circle positive people?

_____
_____
_____
_____

Am I nurturing my relationship with my inner circle?

_____
_____
_____
_____

Insights

_____
_____
_____
_____
_____
_____
_____
_____
_____
_____
_____
_____
_____
_____
_____
_____
_____
_____
_____
_____
_____

MENTAL SELF-CARE

Mental self-care has to do with engaging in activities that relax your mind and allow your mind to grow. We live in a world that's changing and evolving every day. What was in vogue ten years ago is not anymore. I remember when we had hi5 and MySpace. But today we have Facebook and Twitter. Today we have flat-screen smart televisions instead of the hunchback black-and-white televisions.

As the world evolves, you also need to evolve as a person and develop yourself mentally.

Imagine how life will be if you decide not to learn new things. Five years from now, you'll become obsolete like a computer software that wasn't updated by its owner.

As women, we need to engage and grow our minds with activities that build us up mentally like reading a book, solving a puzzle, playing chess, going to a museum, etc. This also includes learning a new skill or hobby, joining a class, a group, or a workshop on a topic that's interesting to you.

The more you develop your mind, the more you will feel enlightened and useful as a person. Also, developing your mind allows you to improve on your set of skills and abilities that increases your value in the long run.

In addition to this, we need to engage in activities that calm our minds and destress us. At the end of a long and stressful day, you must take time to do an activity that calms your mind. You need to unwind.

Journal Activity

What do I do to calm my mind?

_____

_____

_____

_____

_____

What activities stimulate and grow my mind?

_____

_____

_____

_____

_____

How important is it to engage myself mentally
in educational and growth activities?

_____

_____

_____

_____

_____

Insights

_____
_____
_____
_____
_____
_____
_____
_____
_____
_____
_____
_____
_____
_____
_____
_____
_____
_____
_____
_____
_____
_____
_____

SPIRITUAL SELF-CARE

I can't talk about self-care without talking about spirituality. You're made of body, soul, and spirit, so you also need to take care of yourself spiritually.

I believe this is important because you need to develop your spiritual life so you can deepen your meaning of life. You need to connect with God.

Get to know God for yourself instead of just depending on what others have to say. Pray and meditate on the word of God as often as you can. Develop a spiritual care routine. You need to carve out time dedicated to your spirituality every day.

This is very important for Christian women. Joshua 1:8 tells us to meditate on the word of God.

In addition to that, in Luke 10:41–42, Jesus went to visit the two sisters, Mary and Martha. Martha had been busy running around trying to prepare and put logistics together to serve Jesus as he visited them. However, Mary sat at the feet of Jesus to listen to him and learn from him. When Martha complained about why Mary wasn't helping out, Jesus answered and said, "My dear Martha, you are worried and upset over all these details! There is only one thing worth being concerned about.

Mary has discovered it, and it will not be taken away from her."

This is insightful,and shows that as we run around doing everything, we need to also make time for our spirituality.

I know this is so hard to do when you're a busy woman because you feel you're too busy, but we must have a dedicated time for our spiritual nurturing. In addition to your spiritual care time, you can also nurture your spirit as you go about your day.

You can listen to audio scriptures, sermons, or worship music in the background and pray at home or while driving to work, doing your chores, or running some errands. Also read a spiritual book and have fellowship with other Christians often to nurture your spirit.

Every woman must include spirituality in her self-care practice.

Journal Activity

How important is spirituality to my wellness?

_____
_____
_____
_____
_____

What are my spiritual growth activities?

_____
_____
_____
_____
_____

How do I feel when I engage in these
spiritual growth activities?

_____
_____
_____
_____
_____
_____

Insights

EMOTIONAL SELF-CARE

Emotional self-care has to do with your feelings and how you deal with them. Are you emotionally intelligent? Can you understand how you feel and deal with your emotions properly? Are you dealing with your feelings in the right way, or are you harboring your feelings and numbing them with indulgences like alcohol, drugs, food, and shopping, just to mention a few?

You need to develop a healthy coping mechanism for dealing with emotions like anger, anxiety, sadness, fear, etc.

You can deal with negative emotions by committing them to God. The Bible tells us to cast all our anxieties to God because he cares for us (1 Peter 5:7). Philippians 4:6–7 also tells us not to worry about anything:

> Don't worry about anything; instead, pray about everything. Tell God what you need, and thank him for all he has done. Then you will experience God's peace, which exceeds anything we can understand. His peace will guard your hearts and minds as you live in Christ Jesus.

When you find yourself dealing with anxiety, fear, and negative emotions, you need to talk to God and give it all to him because he will work it all out for your good.

After talking to God, you can deal with your emotions by having an objective sounding board— someone to whom you can express your feelings. This person must be trustworthy, God fearing, and able to help you talk through your feelings so you can deal with them in a much more positive and effective way. Examples of positive sounding boards are a life coach, a godly relative, a therapist, a pastor, or a church leader.

Every woman must also include emotional self-care in her self-care practice.

Journal Activity

Am I dealing with my emotions properly?

_____

_____

_____

_____

_____

Who are my trusted people serving
as sounding boards?

_____

_____

_____

_____

What happens when I don't handle
my emotions properly?

_____

_____

_____

_____

Insights

_____
_____
_____
_____
_____
_____
_____
_____
_____
_____
_____
_____
_____
_____
_____
_____
_____
_____
_____
_____
_____
_____

Chapter Four

THE SELF-CARE WHEEL

*N*ow that you know about balanced self-care, I want to introduce to you the self-care wheel. The self-care wheel is an adaptation of the Wheel of Life exercise. The Wheel of Life exercise is a popular coaching assessment tool because it's a simple yet powerful diagnostic tool.

This self-care wheel can be very revealing. The self-care wheel can force you to examine your blind spots and own up to where you need to dramatically improve your self-care routine. The self-care wheel helps you determine the areas of self-care that are lacking in your life so you can make changes and make sure you're taking care of all the vital areas of your life.

Are you neglecting the vital areas of your self-care and focusing on just a few things? When used weekly, monthly, or quarterly, the self-care wheel can help you build positive momentum and make corrections as needed.

Think of the big picture. Self-care is a very important journey, and this is the time you should think about where you are and what areas are lacking in your self-care routine.

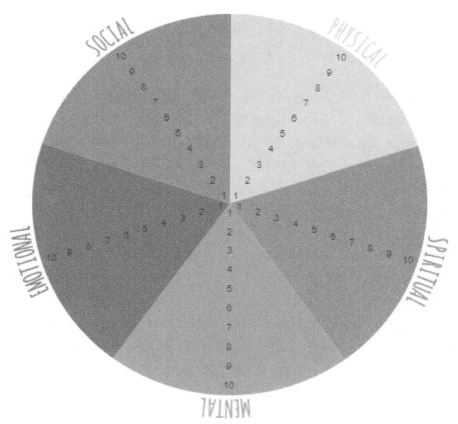

Journal Activity

On a scale of 1 to 10 (1 being the lowest
and 10 being the highest), how satisfied and
fulfilled are you with each area of self-care?

_____

_____

_____

_____

_____

What areas of self-care am I doing presently?

_____

_____

_____

_____

What areas of self-care am I neglecting?

_____

_____

_____

_____

If I don't change my self-care routine, where will I end up in the next three months?

_____

_____

_____

_____

_____

_____

_____

What three things can I implement into my weekly routine to improve my self-care and wellness?

_____

_____

_____

_____

_____

_____

_____

_____

Insights

Chapter Five

THE DRAINS-AND-FILLERS METHOD OF SELF-CARE

We have spent some time in the previous chapters going over the balanced self-care routine and applying it to our lives. In this chapter I want to introduce you to the drains-and-fillers method of self-care.

Ally is a mom who works outside the house from 9 a.m. to 5 p.m. Her work makes her feel drained. She comes home from work and takes care of her kids until they go to bed at 8 p.m. Then she does the house chores. She tries to finish off work projects then goes to bed by 11 p.m. She has this same routine all week. She's exhausted after watching her kids the whole day on Saturdays and Sundays.

Elise is a mom who also works out of the house 9 a.m. to 5 p.m. in a draining job. She comes home to watch her kids until they sleep at 8 p.m. She then does her chores and tries to catch up on her work until 10 p.m. However, she makes sure she spends an hour before bed on an activity that fills her up. She does it consistently from Monday to Sunday.

Which of these two moms do you think will be super drained or burned out at the end of the week?

Obviously, Ally will feel more drained by the end of the week because all the activities in her week were drains. She doesn't make time for activities that fill her up. On the other hand, Elise engages in seven hours of activities that fill her up all week. This may not be ideal, but it's enough to prevent burnout.

Every task or activity that you engage in as a woman either drains you or fills you up. What is a drain to someone may be a filler to another. You need to recognize the activities in your life that drain you and make you feel empty or tired. You also need to recognize people and activities that fill you up and make you replenished or energized at the end of doing them.

You now have to make sure your weekly schedule has enough fillers to help you recuperate after you engage in the draining activities. In short, you need to have the right mix of activities (drains and fillers) so you can achieve inner balance and be more fulfilled.

You need to identify activities and people that fill you up. It could be meditation, taking naps, a relaxing hobby, taking a walk, listening to a podcast, etc. Establishing a strategic refueling plan and consistently using it will go a long way to help you reduce stress.

Journal Activity

Looking at my weekly schedule, what are the drains in my life?

_____

_____

_____

_____

_____

Looking at my weekly schedule, what are the activities that fill me up?

_____

_____

_____

_____

_____

Do I have the right mix of drainers and fillers on my schedule?

_____

_____

_____

_____

Moving forward, how many more filling
activities should I add to my schedule
to replenish my lost energy?

_____

_____

_____

_____

_____

How many hours a day of filling
activities can I commit to weekly?

_____

_____

_____

_____

_____

Where can I fit the filling activities
on my weekly schedule?

_____

_____

_____

_____

_____

Insights

_____
_____
_____
_____
_____
_____
_____
_____
_____
_____
_____
_____
_____
_____
_____
_____
_____
_____
_____
_____
_____
_____

Chapter Six

SELF-CARE: ONE MINUTE AT A TIME

*W*hen you are busy and have no time or money, it's hard to afford or make time for the big things like vacations, spa days, etc. When I started implementing self-care into my routine, I started with taking a mandatory day off every week. I paid someone to watch my kids from 9 a.m. to 5 p.m. so I could take a day off catching up on sleep and doing things for myself that have nothing to do with the kids, chores, or work. That was my "me" time.

After doing this for a month, I started feeling better physically, emotionally, and psychologically. However, I realized paying someone every week was expensive. I couldn't sustain it in the long term, so I needed to find a creative way of implementing a time-saving and affordable self-care routine.

I decided to spread the eight hours I was getting from my day off into one hour a day. My new plan was to get two 15-minute "me" time breaks during the day and 30 minutes to unwind in the evening after the kids go to sleep. This added up to one hour for "me" time a day. This was time for relaxing, putting my feet up, sipping on something cold or warm depending on the weather, reading a book, meditating, watching funny movies, journaling, writing, etc. This nonnegotiable time is for me.

After making this plan, I realized this was easier than I thought it would be. I was now conscious about making some time for myself, so I was seeing the little parts of my day. I was spending time on unnecessary things like social media.

For example, I found I always had about 15 minutes of waiting in the kids' school parking lot. So I decided to use that time as "me" time. I've been practicing this for a while now. I can tell you that it really makes a big difference. It may be a little bit at a time, but it adds up eventually.

In the previous chapters, you have discovered strategies to improve your self-care routine. You may be feeling like you are too busy and can't make time to implement these strategies in your life. My advice to you is to start with baby steps.

You could start with increments of five minutes a day, then work it up to an amount of time that works best for you. A little bit at a time will go a long way to improve your overall wellness.

Journal Activity

How many hours a week will be enough self-care time for me?

_____
_____
_____
_____
_____

Where can I fit this self-care time on my weekly schedule?

_____
_____
_____
_____
_____

What activities will I be doing to fill myself up weekly?

_____
_____
_____
_____
_____

Insights

WRAP-UP

In this section we have gone over what self-care is, why self-care is important, and simple but effective ways of practicing self-care. This may seem like a lot of information, but you have to just create a plan for yourself based on all the strategies I have given. Ask yourself what your ideal self-care plan will look like, what amount of self-care you'll need in each area of self-care, and where you can fit self-care in your schedule.

For I can do everything through Christ, who gives me strength.

PHILIPPIANS 4:13

Part Two

MAKE THE COMMITMENT

Make the commitment to work on your life and apply the insights in this book to your life for the transformation you've been yearning for.

Chapter Seven

MAKE A BOLD DECISION

The first step in creating transformation in your life is deciding to do so. All the self-care insights and strategies shared in part one of this book won't be relevant to you if you don't make a decision to commit to implementing them in your life. Usually, when people start the journey to self-improvement, they immediately start focusing on the results they're seeking before they're fully committed to working toward that result. When it's not as easy as they'd hoped, they get frustrated and give up.

However, when you start your transformational journey with a powerful decision, you prepare yourself to do what it takes to achieve the success you desire and dream of.

DECIDE AND MAKE A COMMITMENT

To decide, as defined by the Merriam-Webster dictionary, is to make a final choice or judgment about something.

In this context, making a decision to commit to the success of your journey to transformation is to make the final choice to succeed no matter what challenges or obstacles you face.

Creating transformation in your life is not an easy thing. You'll face obstacles. There'll be days when you want to give up. You'll be rejected. You'll make some mistakes. Some results may take longer than you expect. At times you'll doubt yourself and your abilities. It's your response to these challenges that determines your success.

If you don't make the bold decision to fully commit to your success, you will lose focus and give up when the going gets tough.

In this phase of your journey to wellness, you want to create your decision statement. Your decision statement will serve as a reminder of why you want to make a change in your life. It'll also give you clarity, motivation, and focus.

Journal Activity

Make a decision to commit to this self-care journey and write it down. Memorize your decision statement. Recite your decision statement daily. Post your decision statement somewhere you can see it.

Ask yourself, "What decision can I make right now that will spur me into action and help me stay committed to this journey of transformation?"

Here's a decision statement example: *I am doing this. I am not giving up! I will do what it takes to build the life that I dream of.*

_____

_____

_____

_____

_____

_____

_____

_____

_____

_____

Insights

_____

_____

_____

_____

_____

_____

_____

_____

_____

_____

_____

_____

_____

_____

_____

_____

_____

_____

_____

_____

_____

_____

_____

_____

_____

_____

Chapter Eight

IDENTIFY YOUR WHY

When I decided to surrender my invisible cape and commit to a life of self-care, I identified two important whys.

My first why was my children. I told myself I want to be the best mom to them and give them all the care they need. I realized I won't be able to do this if I'm not well. I realized I needed to be healthy and strong for them. I realized if I didn't make changes in the way I was treating myself, I may not be able to live and see my kids when they grow up. Therefore, thinking about them even when I lose motivation inspires me to keep working toward my goal.

My second why was my internal joy and fulfillment. I realized stress and overwhelm was taking over my sense of joy and happiness. I wasn't happy, even though I had everything I wanted in life. I decided to choose joy. I realized that when the stress was gone, I felt much happier and stronger to follow my dreams and go after my purpose. When I was stressed, I couldn't write. I kept experiencing writer's block that made me so unfulfilled because I get a lot of fulfillment from writing.

Now, anytime I lose motivation, I remind myself of the place I used to be before I started my self-care journey and what the ultimate goal is. This motivates me to keep practicing self-care.

When you have powerful reasons for being committed to your decision, you'll take the necessary action and not give up even when the going gets tough.

Please identify your why. What is inspiring you to pursue wellness? This will allow you to stay focused and motivate you to keep working on this journey to wellness even when you lose hope.

Journal Activity

Write out all the reasons why you've made this decision.

_____

_____

_____

_____

_____

Why is this self-care journey important to you?

_____

_____

_____

_____

Will it enable you to be the best you can be?

_____

_____

_____

_____

How happy and fulfilled will you feel when you succeed?

_____

_____

_____

_____

_____

_____

_____

_____

_____

How will your success impact others?

_____

_____

_____

_____

_____

_____

_____

_____

_____

_____

_____

Insights

Chapter Nine

WHY WILL YOU SUCCEED?

*N*ow that you have identified why you are embarking on this self-care journey, we want to focus on why you believe you'll succeed. This is a very important part of this journey because it helps you embrace all the reasons why you know you'll succeed and motivates you to focus on the strengths you have.

As a Christian woman, don't forget what Philippians 4:13 says: "For I can do everything through Christ, who gives me strength."

Yes, you can do everything because you have God on your side. God also has put in you so many strengths and abilities that will help you succeed in this journey. So just dig deep and identify all the reasons why you'll succeed.

Here's an example:

I'll succeed in this self-care journey because I'm a child of God, and God will help me. I'm an excellent woman and completely believe in the value of living a balanced life. I really care about myself and my success. I'm a great woman, and my positive, energetic, and motivating personality inspires and encourages me. I have a great attitude. I'm persistent, committed, and motivated. I have supportive friends and family, a great coach, and a network of people who will support me in my journey. Perhaps most importantly, I've already been successful in virtually every major endeavor I've undertaken, starting in high school and continuing on until today.

Journal Activity

Why do you believe you'll have the life of your dreams? Include your skills, talents, education, philosophies, experiences, personal characteristics, support systems, and anything else you can think of. Use complete sentences and the word *I*.

_____

_____

_____

_____

_____

_____

_____

_____

_____

_____

_____

_____

_____

_____

_____

_____

_____

Insights

WRAP-UP: STAY COMMITTED

Now that you have made your bold decision and identified why you want this and why you'll succeed, I want to encourage you to stay committed to the decision you have made today. Speak your decision statement—your *why* statement—into a voice recorder. Listen to it every morning as your words of affirmation. Speak your decision statement out loud. Read your belief narrative regularly.

When you notice that your belief is waning, use it as an opportunity to deepen your commitment. Get in touch with the feelings you had when you initially did these exercises. Your belief, commitment, and confidence will increase.

Then God said, "Let us make human beings in our image, to be like us. They will reign over the fish in the sea, the birds in the sky, the livestock, all the wild animals on the earth, and the small animals that scurry along the ground."

So God created human beings in his own image. In the image of God he created them; male and female he created them.

GENESIS 1:26-27

Part Three

BARRIERS TO SELF-CARE

*As you embark on your self-care journey to more
balance and fulfillment, overcome obstacles
to practicing proper and effective self-care by
using the three key mindset shifts to transform
your life and setting personal boundaries.*

Chapter Ten

CHANGE YOUR SELF-VALUE MINDSET

*T*he first mindset shift you need to make on your journey to wellness is to change your self-value mindset. I always talk about self-value because it's the core of a lot of the things I do as a coach.

A balanced self-esteem is when you capitalize on your strengths, work to overcome the weaknesses you can overcome, and live with the notion that even though you have limitations, you're valuable.

When you value yourself and have a balanced self-esteem, it's so easy for you to take care of yourself. This is because a balanced self-esteem allows you to consider your physical, emotional, and psychological wellness in your decision-making.

When you value yourself, you don't allow others to violate you or take advantage of you. A *balanced self-esteem* makes you confident and not afraid to speak up when you need to.

When something is important to us, we value it and make time for it. We also make sure we take care of our possessions so they don't lose value. That's why you service your car periodically and your HVAC system often. If you own a home, I'm sure you maintain it from time to time so it doesn't depreciate.

You make time for maintaining all these possessions, but you neglect to take care of yourself. Why is that?

If you don't adhere to the maintenance routine suggested by your car's manufacturer, with time your engine may break down, and you may possibly lose your car. Self-care is the maintenance you perform on yourself so you don't break down.

We're so busy placing value on all these inanimate things and putting our time into taking care of them, though in reality we're more important than these things. If you have all these things but you break down because of poor self-care, how will you be able to enjoy them?

Have you forgotten that Genesis 1:26–27 says you're made in the image of God? So why aren't you valuing yourself?

You need to change your self-value mindset. You need to place value on yourself and see yourself as more valuable than any material possessions you may have. You need to make time for maintaining yourself so that you can live to enjoy all your possessions.

Journal Activity

What are my three most valuable assets?

_____

_____

_____

_____

_____

On a scale of 1 to 10, how much energy and effort
do I put into maintaining my most valuable assets?

_____

_____

_____

_____

_____

Do I value myself more than the three
assets mentioned above?

_____

_____

_____

_____

_____

Do I put in as much effort in taking care of myself
as much as I care for these possessions?

_____

_____

_____

_____

_____

What can I do differently?

_____

_____

_____

_____

_____

_____

_____

_____

_____

_____

_____

_____

Insights

_____

_____

_____

_____

_____

_____

_____

_____

_____

_____

_____

_____

_____

_____

_____

_____

_____

_____

_____

_____

_____

_____

Chapter Eleven

SHIFT YOUR SELF-CARE PRIORITIES

I was brought up to always put myself last in everything so I can be selfless and empathetic. Before I had kids, I put God first, my marriage second, my career and ministry third, then myself last.

After I had kids, I switched to putting God first, family second, career and ministry third, and myself last. These priorities are my core values. They also keep me from being self-centered and allow me to sacrifice and give my all to my family and loved ones.

After five years of being a mom, I realized something wasn't right, as I felt so worn out and out of sync. I was sacrificing self-care for the sake of my family.

Little did I know that I need to turn my priorities around as a mom. Of course, God always remains the number one and ultimate priority. However, my self-care needs to be put above the care of anyone else. Therefore, I developed self-care priorities that are different from my core value priorities.

I've realized I need to take care of myself because that's how I can be strong enough to give my best to my family. It's very much like securing your oxygen mask first before you help others in case of an emergency when you're on the plane.

If you can change your self-care priorities and start focusing on your individual physical, mental and emotional needs, you will be able to achieve balance and feel more fulfilled so you can give your best to your family and work.

Practicing self-care as a woman or mom doesn't make you self-centered, selfish, or self-focused. Self-care is rather an opportunity for you to replenish the energy lost from caring for your loved ones. And the more you replenish that energy, the more you can give to the most important people and things in your life.

And remember, self-care is *not* selfish.

Journal Activity

What are the five most important things
to me? Put them in order of priority.

_____

_____

_____

_____

_____

Where am I placing myself on my priority list?

_____

_____

_____

_____

How is my current priority order
affecting my level of self-care?

_____

_____

_____

_____

With this insight, how important is it to put self-care first?

_____

_____

_____

_____

_____

_____

_____

What changes can I make in my priorities so I can make more time for self-care?

_____

_____

_____

_____

_____

_____

_____

_____

_____

_____

_____

_____

Insights

_____
_____
_____
_____
_____
_____
_____
_____
_____
_____
_____
_____
_____
_____
_____
_____
_____
_____
_____
_____
_____
_____
_____
_____

Chapter Twelve

SEE SELF-CARE AS A NECESSITY, NOT A LUXURY

Many of us women see self-care as a luxury, so when we hear self-care, the first thing that comes to mind is a luxurious trip to the spa or a vacation. We also tend to attach money to self-care, so a lot of us don't practice self-care because we feel we can't afford it.

We need to switch our mindset and realize that though spa days and vacations are good forms of self-care, those are just a tiny percentage of all the other self-care routines that a woman can implement in her life.

See self-care as a necessity that you implement in your life so you can replenish the energy that you exert in your day-to-day activities. Also realize that you don't need to spend a lot of money to be able to take care of yourself.

Practicing self-care helps you lower your stress level so you can improve your relationships and interaction with the people close to you. It's a win-win for everyone. Until you change your mindset about self-care, you won't be able to go all out to nurture your physical, spiritual, social, emotional, and psychological well-being.

Journal Activity

How important is self-care to my well-being?

_____

_____

_____

_____

_____

What are the five most important
things to me in order of priority?

_____

_____

_____

_____

_____

Can I put myself first in relation to self-
care, wellness, and well-being?

_____

_____

_____

_____

_____

On a scale of 1 to 10, how much value do I put on myself?

_____

_____

_____

_____

_____

How can I show more love to myself?

_____

_____

_____

_____

_____

_____

_____

_____

_____

_____

_____

_____

_____

_____

_____

_____

Insights

_____

_____

_____

_____

_____

_____

_____

_____

_____

_____

_____

_____

_____

_____

_____

_____

_____

_____

_____

_____

_____

_____

_____

_____

Chapter Thirteen

LEARN TO SAY NO

*M*any of my clients usually join my coaching program feeling very overwhelmed, tired, and almost burned out. Most of the time, after I assess their day-to-day activities, I find that they're busy doing things for other people without considering their wellness.

Usually these clients say it's so hard for them to say no to people when they ask for help. Therefore, they end up saying yes to everyone's request and making commitments that are very hard to follow through.

WHY IT'S HARD TO SAY NO

Some women admit they can't say no because they fear rejection. They're usually scared the other party will get upset and thus reject them in the future. Therefore, to not upset their friends, loved ones, and bosses, they stretch themselves thin to please them. In addition, they can't say no because they want to preserve their relationships with them.

Some women also can't say no to requests from people because they're afraid they'll be judged as wicked, selfish, and proud. Others also lack the confidence to say no even after they've rehearsed it over and over again.

CONSEQUENCES OF NOT SAYING NO TO OTHERS WHEN NECESSARY

The consequences of not being able to say no to demands from others are overwhelm and burnout. In addition, the inability of some people to follow through with commitments they've made to certain friends and loved ones result in broken relationships.

Also, people who can't say no sometimes come across as untrustworthy and incompetent because they take on responsibilities but can't fulfill them according to the expectations of the people who asked for their help.

Furthermore, when people can't say no when they need to, they tend to feel unfulfilled and used at the end of the day. This is because they neglect themselves in their bid to please others, thereby overstretching their capabilities and feeling drained in the end.

There are times when saying no is necessary. If the request violates your personal principles, you must say no. If you're being asked to do something that's way above your limits in terms of capacity, capability, and schedule, you must say no. Lack of boundaries and not being able to say no is one of the biggest hindrances and challenges you may face as you start to practice self-care.

Insights

Chapter Fourteen

STRATEGIES FOR SAYING NO

$\mathcal{I}$ n this chapter, I will share with you some simple but effective strategies for saying no. By implementing these strategies, you will be more equipped to say no when necessary.

SET REASONABLE BOUNDARIES.

The first strategy for saying no easily is to set boundaries. I believe that unconsciously, we all have our limits on how far we can go without feeling too overstretched and drained in the end. You must therefore set reasonable boundaries and stick to them.

For example, when I was working in the corporate world, Sundays were the days I absolutely needed off. That was a boundary I set for myself. Therefore, in every position I held, I let people know I couldn't work on Sundays. They respected those boundaries and made sure not to schedule me for Sundays.

Regarding certain important things like work schedule, volunteering, helping others on projects, sleep time, and the number of hours worked, you also need to set boundaries even before you get requests from people.

When you set boundaries, you must think about the consequences of crossing the boundaries. For instance, being a mom, there's no way I can work more than a certain number of hours a day. Therefore, when I schedule clients, I always have in mind the number of clients I can book in a day. This boundary allows me to say no to clients when they want to book certain times. Even though it's hard sometimes, I know the consequences of crossing my limit are stress and overwhelm. As soon as I think about the negative consequences of crossing my boundaries, I get confident about saying no to requests from clients.

Therefore, set boundaries for yourself about how much time and effort you have to offer to others by putting into consideration your own responsibilities and priorities first. Make sure you have taken care of your priorities before you accept responsibilities from others.

DON'T BE AGGRESSIVE. BE ASSERTIVE.

A lot of people think saying no must be done aggressively so the other party can understand how serious they are. However, my experience has shown me that when you avoid the aggressive path and take the assertive way of saying no, people tend to understand you better and reason with you.

Don't be rude, offensive, abusive, or impatient. Instead, say no in a clear and understandable way while caring about the other person's feelings. For example, instead of saying, "No, it's not possible," you can say, "I'd be happy to help, but unfortunately, I can't help you at this time. I apologize."

Being assertive allows you to express yourself politely so that the other person understands your point of view and feels you understand them too. This simple strategy for saying no to others will go a long way to help you become more expressive of yourself and communicate what works for you in a simple and nice way.

REPLACE THE USUAL QUICK YES WITH "I'LL THINK ABOUT IT."

A lot of women who struggle with saying no when needed usually give their answer too quickly. They sometimes feel pressured to respond immediately to the person making the request. However, you need to have it in mind that you are not obliged to give a response immediately if you aren't sure.

I struggle a lot with this myself. I realize that when I rush to answer, I tend to regret it after I've had the chance to think things through. Usually I would've already made the commitment and couldn't go back on my word.

Therefore, replace your usual quick yes with "I'll think about it." When you do this, it gives you the chance to actually think things through before you make any commitments to someone. This allows you to weigh the pros and cons of the situation to make the best decision.

DON'T BE AFRAID OF PEOPLE'S REACTIONS.

When you say no to someone's request, they either react in a positive or negative way. Usually people who react in negative ways would try to make you feel bad for not being able to give them what they are looking for. When people don't get their way, they usually react negatively.

But please don't feel bad. People's reactions are beyond your control, and making an informed decision that's not in their favor doesn't make you a bad person. I always say we can't be everything to everyone. Therefore, if something is going to affect you negatively and make you overstretch yourself, don't be afraid to express your unavailability to fulfill someone's desire.

OFFER AN ALTERNATIVE.

The last strategy for saying no to others when needed is to offer an alternative. Objective people are usually open to alternatives to their requests. Therefore, if you genuinely want to say yes to someone but find it's not possible to do so exactly as the person is requesting, you can go ahead and politely let them know you're happy to help in another way if they're open to that.

Doing this allows the person to see that you have a genuine heart to help. It also gives the opportunity for the person to decide if what works for you is an alternative for them or not.

In conclusion, saying no is something that we all have to consistently work on. It gets better by the day. It's very important to be able to say no to others when necessary because it allows you to regulate your responsibility loads, reduces your level of stress, and prevent burnout.

Journal Activity

Is it hard for me to say no?

_____
_____
_____
_____
_____
_____
_____
_____
_____

Why is it challenging for me to say no?

_____
_____
_____
_____
_____
_____
_____
_____
_____
_____

How does my inability to say no affect my wellness?

_____

_____

_____

_____

_____

_____

_____

_____

_____

What strategies will I be implementing in
my life to make saying no a lot easier?

_____

_____

_____

_____

_____

_____

_____

_____

Insights

WRAP-UP

In this section of the book, we've discussed three important mindset shifts you need to make and how you can set the right boundaries so you can prevent responsibility overload. I hope for you that you can arm yourself with these strategies so that you can overcome any mindset blocks or challenges that may hinder your progress as you continue to work on your health and wellness.

OUTRO: I BELIEVE IN YOU

In this book I've prepared you for your self-care journey by helping you identify simple but effective strategies you can implement in your everyday life so you can unwind, destress, and live a more balanced, fulfilling, and joyous life.

I'm so happy you've made it this far. You have no idea how happy I am about the journey you're about to undertake.

You may be overwhelmed by all the information I've given you in this book, but you get to decide which of these ideas are relevant to your life so you can implement them.

Don't rush your transformation. Take it one day at a time. Whenever you feel like giving up, just remember that *you* can do all things through Christ who strengthens you. Times will come when you think *you* are not making any progress, but just don't give up and keep pushing. God will work it all out for good.

I'll be thrilled to hear about your self-care journey and be part of it. If you need help with implementing these self-care strategies into your life, I'm delighted to work with you. I'm offering you one free 30-minute self-care strategy session with me. We'll delve into your current situation, your obstacles, and ways you can move forward so you can implement a self-care routine that would help you live a more balanced and burnout-free life.

Book your free session with me at
https://www.empoweredforbalance.com/freesession

REFERENCE

Babcock, Elisabeth D. 2014. *Using Brain Science to Design New Pathways Out of Poverty*. PDF. Boston: Crittenton Women's Union. https://s3.amazonaws.com/empath-website/pdf/Research-UsingBrainScienceDesignPathwaysPoverty-0114.pdf.

ABOUT THE AUTHOR

Ama Brew is an author, a certified life coach, a keynote speaker, and a human resources consultant. Combining her BA in psychology, master's degree in organizational leadership & human resource management, life coach training, and personal experience, Ama delivers a personalized coaching experience to help her life coaching clients gain more control in their lives, achieve balance, and design the lives they were meant to live: fulfilled, confident, joyful, and free from what has been holding them back.

Following a rewarding career as a human resources manager, Ama went on to develop a childcare business to be fully involved in the daily care of her children. She became so committed to the care of her kids that she lost herself for years.

She found her way back to a balanced and purposeful life and is now on a mission to help other women who are experiencing the taxing demands of balancing motherhood, caring for a home, and a professional life.

Ama founded and developed Empowered for Balance for that purpose and today works with women who are spinning multiple plates and looking for more fulfillment, purpose, and balance in their lives. Ama delves into the root cause of the imbalance in her client's lives to educate, empower, and coach them to transform so they too can live more balanced and purposeful lives.

Ama supports her husband in ministry in New Hampshire, USA. She and her husband are parents to a beautiful daughter and two adorable twin boys.

Connect with Ama at the following links:

WEBSITE
https://www.empoweredforbalance.com

FACEBOOK
https://www.facebook.com/empoweredforbalance

INSTAGRAM
https://www.instagram.com/empoweredforbalance

PINTEREST
https://www.pinterest.com/empoweredforbalance

Printed in Great Britain
by Amazon